I0888906

STARTING OUT

CREATIVE EDUCATION • CREATIVE PAPERBACKS

PUBLISHED BY CREATIVE EDUCATION AND CREATIVE PAPERBACKS
P.O. Box 227, Mankato, Minnesota 56002
Creative Education and Creative Paperbacks are imprints of The Creative Company
www.thecreativecompany.us

LIBRARY OF CONGRESS CATALOGING-IN-PUBLICATION DATA
Names: Riggs, Kate, author.
Title: Baby elephants / Kate Riggs.
Series: Starting out.
Summary: A baby elephant narrates the story of its life, describing how physical features, diet, habitat, and familial relationships play a role in its growth and development.

Identifiers: ISBN 978-1-64026-074-0 (hardcover)
ISBN 978-1-62832-662-8 (pbk)
ISBN 978-1-64000-190-9 (eBook)
This title has been submitted for CIP processing under LCCN 2018939103.

CCSS: RI.K.1, 2, 3, 4, 5, 6, 7; RI.1.1, 2, 3, 4, 5, 6, 7; RF.K.1, 3; RF.1.1

DESIGN AND PRODUCTION
by Chelsey Luther and Joe Kahnke
Art direction by Rita Marshall
Printed in the United States of America

PHOTOGRAPHS by Alamy (Arterra Picture Library, Bailey-Cooper Photography, blickwinkel, Martin Harvey), Dreamstime (Duncan Noakes, Chinnasorn Pangcharoen), Getty Images (Digital Zoo/DigitalVision, Matej Divizna/Getty Images News, Gallo Images - Michael Poliza/Riser, Alexander Yates/Moment), iStockphoto (Riaan Coetzee, EcoPic, rusm), Minden Pictures (Richard Du Toit, Anup Shah/NPL), Shutterstock (Aroonsak, Bohbeh), SuperStock (Ferrero Labat/Pantheon)

FIRST EDITION HC 9 8 7 6 5 4 3 2 1
FIRST EDITION PBK 9 8 7 6 5 4 3 2 1

baby ELEPHANTS

KATE RIGGS

CONT

ENTS

I AM A CALF.

I am a baby elephant.

Look at my wrinkly skin!

I weighed about 200 pounds (90.7 kg) at birth.

My mother fed me food. I have a trunk. But what does it do?

My herd is my family. I have many older siblings, cousins, and aunts.

Everyone takes
care of each other.

My teeth and tusks are growing. The first set will fall out in a year. Then new teeth will come in.

I will drink milk for two years. My teeth will help me eat plants.

Now I know what to do with my trunk! It helps me hold onto things.

We are always on the move. We remember where to find water.

Elephants need a lot of food! I dig up roots with my tusks. I find grasses and fruits.

It is hot where I live. I take a bath in the mud.

I am
a young
elephant
now!

SPEAK AND LISTEN

TOOOOT!

Can you speak like a calf? Elephants trumpet with their trunks. They also rumble.

Listen to these sounds:
https://news.nationalgeographic.com/news/2014/05/what-elephant-calls-mean/

Now it is your turn!

CALF WORDS

herd: a group of animals that live and feed together

siblings: brothers or sisters

trunk: a long nose that can grasp objects

tusks: long, pointed teeth that extend from the mouth

READING CORNER

Bell, Samantha S. *Meet a Baby Elephant*. Minneapolis: Lerner, 2016.

Kelley, K. C. *Baby Elephants*. North Mankato, Minn.: Amicus, 2018.

Niver, Heather Moore. *How Elephants Grow Up*. New York: Enslow, 2017.

INDEX